Bibliographical Series
of Supplements to 'British Book News'
on Writers and Their Work

★

GENERAL EDITOR
Geoffrey Bullough

SIR JOHN VANBRUGH

by

BERNARD HARRIS

PUBLISHED FOR
THE BRITISH COUNCIL
AND THE NATIONAL BOOK LEAGUE
BY LONGMANS, GREEN & CO

LONGMANS GREEN & CO LTD
48 Grosvenor Street, London, W.1

*Associated companies, branches and
representatives throughout the world*

First published 1967
© Bernard Harris 1967

*Printed in Great Britain by
F. Mildner & Sons, London, E.C.1*

176440|05|1

CONTENTS

ILLUSTRATIONS

¶ Sir John Vanbrugh was born in London on 24 January 1664, and died in London on 26 March 1726.

SIR JOHN VANBRUGH

I. THE MODEL OF THE MIND

K NELLER'S portrait of Vanbrugh is worth consideration, for it is the best form of introduction to both a man and a moment.

The man was about forty, a successful comic dramatist and sometime soldier, recently turned architect, created a herald and appointed Comptroller of the Board of Works. These careers meet on canvas as easily as they did in his person. Self-command braces the indolent pose; a satirical gaze checks the heaviness of the face; the casually worn medal of Clarenceux King-at-Arms mocks the professional men from whom the office was won; the dividers are lightly held.

The moment was as privileged as the man. In 1703, during the absence abroad of Jacob Tonson, printer and founder of the Kit Cat Club, Vanbrugh fitted up a room in Tonson's house, Barn Elms, Surrey, for future meetings of the club, and Kneller undertook to adorn its walls with portraits of their fellow-members. Both affairs were in a radiant muddle by mid-June, when Vanbrugh wrote to Tonson in Amsterdam:[1]

Sr Godfrey has been most in fault. The fool has got a country house near Hampton Court, and is so busy about fitting it up (to receive nobody), that there is no getting him to work. Carpenter Johns, too is almost as bad. I went up yesterday under a tylt (as everybody has done that has gone by water these three weeks, for the Devils in the sky); there's all in disorder still; every room is chips—up to your chin!

The disorder within was matched by nature's disarray:

Neighbour Burgess has been too honest; the pease and beans ly all anguishing upon the earth; not a cod has been gathered. There will be a

[1]Quotations from letters and plays are taken from *The Works of Sir John Vanbrugh*, 4 vols, ed. B. Dobrée and G. Webb (1927).

hundred thousand apricocks ripe in ten days; they are now fairer and forwarder than what I saw at the Queens table at Windsor on Sunday— and such strawberrys as never were tasted: currants red as blood to; and gooseberrys, peaches, pairs, apples, and plumbs to gripe the gutts of a nation.

The vivid phrasing of this plea for Tonson to come home is part of the special appeal of Vanbrugh's world, that paradise running to seed, where evil manifested itself most obviously in the English weather, and punishment was consequent upon an appetite for fruit; it was a world of convivial human energy and prodigal bounty, and possessed, in a Shakespearean expression, 'double vigour, art and nature'.

Kneller's pictures no longer hang in 'Jovial Jacob's academic room', but in the National Portrait Gallery. Here it is still possible

by turns in breathing paint to trace
The Wits gay Air, or Poet's genial face.[1]

Vanbrugh, Garth and Congreve—Pope's 'the three most honest-hearted, real good men of the poetical members of the Kit Cat Club'—keep company with Addison and Steele. Yet the club's atmosphere was scarcely literary, despite Tonson's inspiration, and in the first years of the eighteenth century it was a meeting place for Whigs of diverse character and power. Devoted to tippling, mutton-pies, toastings and light verse, the Kit Cats shared a determination to preserve the Protestant cause and secure the Hanoverian succession. Among them were the Earl of Halifax, sometime Chancellor of the Exchequer; the Earl of Carlisle, twice First Lord of the Treasury; the Dukes of Manchester and Newcastle; Viscount Cobham; Robert Walpole, the ascendant politician of that era; and John Churchill, Duke of Marlborough, its military hero.

[1]William Collins, *Drafts and Fragments of Verse*, ed. J. S. Cunningham (1956), p.21.

Halifax and Manchester were patrons of Vanbrugh's theatrical career, and his name as an architect is inseparable from such great houses as Castle Howard, built for Carlisle, Kimbolton, Claremont and Stowe, where Manchester, Newcastle and Cobham employed him respectively. Blenheim Palace, the nation's tribute to Marlborough, became Vanbrugh's most celebrated endeavour, and only through Walpole's intervention was he paid for it. But Vanbrugh's relationships with patrons and clients were fuller than such terms imply, and were neatly expressed in Rowe's verses on 'The Reconcilement between Jacob Tonson and Mr Congreve':

> I'm in with captain Vanburgh at the present,
> A most *sweet-natur'd* gentleman, and pleasant;
> He writes your comedies, draws schemes, and models,
> And builds dukes' houses upon very odd hills:
> For him, so much I dote on him, that I
> If I were sure to go to heaven, would die.

Vanbrugh made his way to fame in that brilliant society—whether as Captain Vanbrugh, the soldier playwright, along with Captain Steele and Captain Farquhar, as Brother Van, the clubman and wit, or as Sir John Vanbrugh, architect of genius—because his nature proved so eminently capable of entertaining, evoking and exhibiting his age's tastes for both comedy and grandeur.

John Vanbrugh was christened on 24 January 1664 at his father's house in the parish of St Nicholas Acon. To this area of merchant activity his grandfather, Gillis van Brugg of Ghent, had fled from Alva's persecution, changed nationality, married an Englishwoman, and set about recreating a dynasty whose ancestors had included a Praetor of Ypres in 1383. Giles, their second son, married Elizabeth Barker, daughter of Sir Dudley Carleton, and John was the first surviving son of their nineteen children.

By 1667 Giles Vanbrugh had set up as a sugar-baker in Chester, where he developed a sound business, kept company with religious dissenters, and concocted an unstable plan for the sack of Rome and the theft of the Vatican Library. John seems to have inherited something of this ambitious spirit, but he displayed a life-long contempt for churchmen and for the provident virtues of tradesmen.

Nothing is known of his education and early life, until he was commissioned in the Earl of Huntingdon's Foot Regiment on 30 January 1686, only to resign in August. At his father's death, in July 1689, John received a competence.

In the summer of 1690 Vanbrugh was arrested at Calais, kept there nine months until his health suffered, transferred at his own cost to Vincennes, near Paris, in May 1691, and early in 1692, with two other Englishmen, was imprisoned in the Bastille on the orders of Louis XIV. It was variously reported that he had been spying out the fortifications of Calais, and that he had been informed against by a woman in Paris for attempting to leave France in wartime without a passport. Vanbrugh hinted to Tonson years later that his own stay in Paris had had a romantic origin. Whatever the true cause it is clear that Vanbrugh and his companions were used in the complicated game of bartering prisoners; he was parolled in November 1692 and came home.

After a spell as an auditor for the Southern Division of Lancaster, Vanbrugh was next commissioned in Lord Berkeley's Marine Regiment of Foot in 1696, served until it was disbanded in 1698, and was still petitioning for pay arrears in 1702 when he became a captain in a new regiment raised by his first commander, the Earl of Huntingdon.

While in the Bastille Vanbrugh drafted part of a comedy, and at some period in his military life when, according to Cibber, 'he was but an ensign, and had a heart above his income', he had been helped by Sir Thomas Skipwith, a Patentee of the Theatre Royal, Drury Lane. The theatrical conditions of the time soon enabled Vanbrugh to repay with his talents as a playwright debts incurred as a soldier.

The decade 1695 to 1705, in which all Vanbrugh's plays appeared, was a time of theatre disputes involving the break-up and re-uniting of companies. In 1695, after a quarrel over the management ethics of Christopher Rich, (Skipwith's fellow patentee) Thomas Betterton, the greatest actor of the day, withdrew from the Theatre Royal, together with most of the experienced players, and opened the new theatre in Lincoln's Inn Fields with Congreve's *Love for Love*. To assist the embarrassed Theatre Royal company Colley Cibber turned playwright with *Love's Last Shift* in 1696, for which Vanbrugh supplied a sequel, *The Relapse, or Virtue in Danger*. Written in six weeks it became the success of the following season. During the intervening months Vanbrugh made a free adaptation of Boursault's *Les Fables d'Ésope* as a two-part *Aesop*, produced in 1697; but despite a topical scene about the current theatre quarrel the play was unsuccessful. Vanbrugh surrendered his profits on these plays and presumably met his obligation to Skipwith.

He next completed his Bastille comedy as *The Provok'd Wife*, and gave it to Lincoln's Inn Fields where its first performance in May 1697, with Betterton as Sir John Brute and Mrs Barry as Lady Brute, brought Vanbrugh immediate triumph and notoriety. It was in the following year that Jeremy Collier's vehement indictment of the contemporary theatre, *A Short View of the Immorality and Profaneness of the English Stage*, made the work of Vanbrugh and Congreve major exhibits. The controversy did not impede Vanbrugh's engagement in theatrical affairs, however, for he adapted Dancourt's farce *La Maison de Campagne*, as *The Country House*, in 1698, and welcomed the new century with a version of Fletcher's *The Pilgrim*, to which Dryden contributed a prologue, epilogue and *A Secular Masque*, whose theme of resolute farewell to the past age was made poignant by Dryden's death.

In 1701, although commenced as an architect, Vanbrugh expediently adapted Dancourt's version of Le Sage's adaptation of Francisco de Rojas Zorilla's *La Traicion busca el castigo*, as *The False Friend*, for Drury Lane, and in 1704 joined with Congreve and Walsh in a translation of Molière's *Monsieur de Pourceaugnac*, as *Squire Trelooby*, for Lincoln's Inn Fields.

Vanbrugh sought to unite his skills in architecture and drama. He reported to Tonson in 1703 that he had given £2,000 for 'the second Stable Yard going up the Haymarket', as a site for a new theatre to be managed by Congreve and himself as a house for Betterton's company. When Queen Anne approved the enterprise as part of a policy for improving the moral tone of the stage, the Society for the Reformation of Manners vainly petitioned the Bishop of London against the prospect of Vanbrugh as manager of the new morality. Nevertheless, The Queen's Theatre, or Italian Opera House, opened on Easter Monday 1705 with Greber's *The Loves of Ergasto*, for which Garth supplied a prologue containing an ironic prophecy, 'When marble fails, the muses' structures live'. The occasion was greeted with hostility by opponents of the political establishment. Defoe's *Review* of 3 May 1705 sarcastically compared 'the Ornament and Magnificence of its Building' with the 'Great Zeal of our Nobility and Gentry, to the Encouragement of Learning, and the Suppressing of Vice and Immorality'. *The Rehearsal of Observator* of 5 May 1705 was minatory:

The Kit-Cat Club is now grown Notorious all over the Kingdom. And they have built a Temple for their Dagon, the new Play-House in the Hay-Market.

Little is actually known of the temple that Cibber called a 'vast triumphal Piece of Architecture', and of whose majestic features he pertinently asked:

what could their vast columns, their gilded cornices, their immoderate high roofs avail, where scarce one word in ten could be distinctly heard in it?

Vanbrugh was unsuccessful as a theatre-designer, and premature, as a theatre manager, in his interest in Italian opera.

He fared no better as a property developer, for though he had confided to Tonson that he expected to be 'reimburs'd every penny for it, by the Spare ground', the purchase of the Haymarket site proved a financial burden to Vanbrugh for years. When Congreve sensibly withdrew from the venture, Vanbrugh could no longer sustain the double task: despite the success of *The Confederacy*, adapted from Dancourt's *Les Bourgeoises a la Mode* in 1705, Vanbrugh ended his practical theatre career with a version of Molière's *Le Dépit Amoureux*, aptly titled *The Mistake*, in the same year.

A verse squib in Defoe's *Review* had already asked a difficult question:

> thus have their first Essays
> *Reform'd* their *Buildings*, not *Reform'd* their *Plays*.
> The Donor's Bounty may be well Design'd,
> But who can Guess the Model of the Mind?

Marlborough's victory at Blenheim in 1704 had determined Vanbrugh's future; he was appointed Surveyor for the building of Blenheim Palace in 1705. Strong in political favour he went in the capacity of Garter King-at-Arms to Hanover in 1706 to invest the future King George I with that order: Vanbrugh was the first knight created on George's Accession in 1714. He resigned from the Surveyorship in 1716 after years of delay, frustration, political dissension, and the enduring hostility of the Duchess of Marlborough. It was Vanbrugh's final humiliation to be shut out from the gates of Blenheim, and to know that his Tory enemies rejoiced that the 'Dutchman may not visit his own child'. The occasion was the more bitter in that Vanbrugh had brought along his wife to see his grandest work and share his biggest snub.

Vanbrugh's marriage was a late, yet characteristic remodelling of his mind. On Boxing Day 1718 he wrote from Castle Howard:

There has now fallen a Snow up to ones Neck .... In short, tis so bloody Cold, I have almost a mind to Marry to keep myself warm.

On 14 January 1719 he married Henrietta Maria, eldest child of James Yarborough, of Heslington Hall, York, a former Lieutenant Colonel of Horse and aide-de-camp to Marlborough. Vanbrugh was fifty-five, Henrietta twenty-six. His courtship attracted notice, and his marriage speculation, for in a celebrated letter Lady Mary Wortley Montagu mentioned:

our York lovers (strange monsters, you'll think, love being as much forced up here as melons). In the first form of these creatures is even Mr Vanbrugh. Heaven, no doubt, compassionating our dulnes, has inspired him with a passion that makes us all ready to die with laughing: 'tis credibly reported that he is endeavouring at the honourable state of matrimony, and vows to lead a single life no more . . . . his inclinations to ruins has given him a fancy for Mrs Yarborough: he sighs and ogles so, that it would do your heart good to see him.[1]

The registers of St James Church, York, record, on one page, Vanbrugh's marriage entry, the burial of Anne, James Yarborough's wife, on 20 April 1718, and the baptism of Anne, James Yarborough's daughter, on 10 May 1718. It seems unlikely that even Vanbrugh courted the pregnant wife of his future father-in-law; probably Lady Mary, once the infant toast of the Kit Cats, was an avid spectator of a military exercise in diversion.

Vanbrugh feared the loss of bachelorhood like a gallant in a play, and six months after 'this great Leap in the Dark, Marriage', as he quoted his own line to Tonson, held that marriage 'was fitter to end Our Life, than begin it'. He kept up a bluff defence against domesticity:

I am now two Boys Strong in the Nursery but am forbid getting any more this Season for fear of killing my Wife. A Reason; that in Kit Cat days, wou'd have been stronger for it, than against it: But let her live, for she's Special good, as far as I know of the Matter.

The robust confidence was misplaced. Only one of their three children survived infancy, Carlisle's godson Charles,

[1] *Letters and Works of Lady Mary Wortley Montagu* (1837), Vol. I, p.155.

who was killed at Fontenoy in 1745 and buried at Ath in his ancestors' country. But the pious wish was granted, for Henrietta outlived her husband by fifty years. Among her papers is part of a letter by Vanbrugh, describing a stay at Castle Howard in 1721, doubtless returned to her because of a passage about Charles's popularity with Carlisle's daughters, Lady Irwin and Lady Mary Howard, who

was as fond of him as she, going twenty times a day into the Nursery, and sitting an hour together by her self, at the Cradle feet, to see him sleep; then carrying him about in her arms as long as she was able, from whence he was handed from one to an other round the family of all Degrees, and a Favourite every where, because he never cry'd.[1]

Vanbrugh died, choked by a quinzey, in his Whitehall house on 26 March 1726, and was buried in the family vault at Wren's church of St Stephen Walbrook. He left an unfinished play, *A Journey to London*, which Cibber completed as *The Provok'd Husband:* thus, a compliment was returned, and comedy extinguished.

II. A MATCHLESS SPIRIT OF IMPUDENCE

Cibber's *Love's Last Shift, or The Fool in Fashion*, dominated by his own performance as Sir Novelty Fashion, had been a comedy of manners that turned into a drama of sentiment. In it the dissolute Loveless, a wife-deserter and debt-evader, returned from overseas to find his loyal wife Amanda conveniently an heiress, and virtue unexpectedly profitable.

Vanbrugh's sequel raised Sir Novelty to the peerage as Lord Foppington, but introduced fresh perspectives by means of the sub-plot which takes the action out of London and describes the pursuit by Lord Foppington's younger

[1]Unpublished letter, quoted by permission of Mrs Norah Gurney, Archivist, The Borthwick Institute of Historical Research, York.

brother of the heiress Miss Hoyden, daughter of Sir Tunbelly Clumsey.

The theme of the rake reformed was not one that Vanbrugh endorsed, and the first scene of *The Relapse* shows Loveless proposing to Amanda a test of his newly-acquired virtue. He intends to return to town. The risks are clear to her and to us, and Amanda's prudence in refraining from pressing her anxieties overbearingly upon Loveless makes us sympathize with this study of precarious love.

Vanbrugh's attitude to love is perhaps close to Loveless's ideal:

> The largest Boons that Heaven thinks fit to grant
> To Things it has decreed shall crawl on Earth,
> Are in the Gift of Women form'd like you.
> Perhaps, when Time shall be no more,
> When the aspiring Soul shall take its flight,
> And drop this pond'rous Lump of Clay behind it,
> It may have Appetites we know not of,
> And pleasures as refin'd as its Desires . . .
> But till that Day of Knowledge shall instruct me,
> The utmost Blessing that my Thought can reach,
> *Taking her in his Arms*
> Is folded in my Arms, and rooted in my Heart.   (I.i)

'There let it grow for ever,' replies Amanda. It is a modest acceptance of a realistic view of love, whose fears and raptures are devotedly human. Vanbrugh's ear for both is sensitive without false artifice. Loveless cruelly persuades Amanda to force him to tantalize her with an anecdote revealing both his confidence in his relationship with her and his longing to talk about another woman:

Loveless. Know then, I happen'd in the Play to find my very Character, only with the Addition of a *Relapse;* which struck me so, I put a suddain stop to a most harmless Entertainment, which till then, diverted me between the Acts. 'Twas to admire the workmanship of Nature, in the Face of a young Lady, that sat some distance from me, she was so exquisitely handsome.

Amanda.   So exquisitely handsome!

Loveless.   Why do you repeat my words, my Dear?

Amanda.   Because you seem'd to speak 'em with such pleasure, I thought I might oblige you with their Eccho.

Loveless.   Then you are allarmed, *Amanda*?

Amanda.   It is my Duty to be so, when you are in danger.

Loveless.   You are too quick in apprehending for me; all will be well when you have heard me out.   (II.i)

Such easy words accomplish more in the theatre than on the page. The audience is drawn into a relationship, familiarly comic yet tense. Amanda is both disturbed and sophisticated enough to engage in a game which offers no consolation to its losers. That she might lose becomes clear when the distracting theatre-goer turns out to be her smart, widowed cousin, Berinthia, who complacently accepts Loveless's ardour and diagnozes his malady, ''Tis the Plague, and we shall all be infected'. When Worthy stumbles upon their association the infection spreads rapidly, for he persuades Berinthia, his former mistress, to help him corrupt Amanda. Vanbrugh is sufficiently unsentimental to let one attack succeed; and sufficiently idealistic to contain the other. In a scene of licentious permissiveness Loveless seduces Berinthia, who cries, 'Help, help, I'm Ravish'd, ruin'd, undone. O Lord, I shall never be able to bear it. (*Very softly*).' (IV.iii)

The quiet outrage sweeps us along with something of Berinthia's composure, because Vanbrugh never allows gratuitous moral instruction to hinder the progress of physical desire, or the comic presentation of appetite.

Lord Foppington is a character richly gathered up from some of the follies of social attitudes in the time. He finds it 'an unspeakable pleasure to be a Man of Quality—Strike me dumb', and that 'the Ladies were ready to pewke at me, whilst I had nothing but Sir Navelty to recommend me to 'em—Sure whilst I was but a Knight, I was a very nauseous Fellow'. Behind Foppington's acceptance of his pose as a beau is a shrewd determination to exploit his ten thousand pounds inheritance, and a self-sufficiency which belies his decorous inanity. He courts Amanda as an exercise in the town's games, and affects dismay at her pretence to literary culture:

Far to mind the inside of a Book, is to entertain ones self with the forc'd Product of another Man's Brain. Naw I think a Man of Quality and Breeding may be much diverted with the Natural Sprauts of his own.

But for all his privileged confidence he becomes a butt. His suit to Amanda ends disastrously, pricked by his own sword. His pride is humiliated when his younger brother impersonates him at Sir Tunbelly's house, secretly marries the heiress, and has him put in a dog kennel.

In the matching of Young Fashion with Miss Hoyden Vanbrugh unites the comic themes of cynical fortune-hunting and self-gratification. Fashion does not mind whom he marries so long as he acquires money; Miss Hoyden is equally indifferent about her husband, so long as he enables her to reach the haven of social freedom and individual liberation. The wish is not empty-headed but full-bodied:

It's well I have a Husband a coming, or Icod, I'd marry the Baker, I wou'd so. No body can knock at the Gate, but presently I must be lockt up; and here's the young Greyhound Bitch can run loose about the House all the day long, she can; 'tis very well. (III.iv)

The longing for an unconstrained life, which so many of Vanbrugh's characters display, is a state which the author sportingly approved and sometimes releases, with a spirited and licentious abandon. Young Fashion, charmed by Miss Hoyden's eager acceptance of him, soliloquizes, in affection-ate but wide-eyed indulgence, about their future life:

I shall have a fine time on't with her in *London;* I'm much mistaken, if she don't prove a *March* Hare all the year round. What a scamp'ring Chace will she make on't when she finds the whole Kennel of Beaux at her Tail! (IV.i)

When the golden prospect is threatened, the counsel of Coupler (the professional match-maker), is effective because, whereas Fashion thinks of the Chaplain and the Nurse as 'The Devil and the Witch', the older man knows that 'we must find what stuff they are made of'. By playing upon the chaplain's real material needs, holding out a rich living and the added benefit of enforced marriage to the Nurse as a means of satisfying his conscience over the concealed marriage, Coupler and Young Fashion enable the clergyman to submit to providence and reconcile flesh and spirit.

In Vanbrugh's comedy animal demands continually assail human feeling. The relationship between the Nurse and Miss Hoyden has none of the bawdy tenderness of Shakespeare's Nurse for Juliet; the earliest memory of Miss Hoyden which her Nurse confides to Fashion is unadorned:

alas, all I can boast of is, I gave her pure good Milk, and so your Honour wou'd have said, an you had seen how the poor thing suck't it—Eh, God's Blessing on the sweet Face on't; how it us'd to hang at this poor Tett, and suck and squeeze, and kick and sprawl it wou'd, till the Belly on't was so full, it wou'd drop off like a Leech. (IV.i)

Miss Hoyden, humiliated by 'a fiddlecome Tale of a draggle-tail'd Girl', urges 'don't tell him what one did then, tell him what one can do now'. Equally frankly, Berinthia tries to persuade Amanda that 'In matters of Love, Men's Eyes are always bigger than their Bellies. They have violent Appetites, 'tis true; But they have soon din'd'. When Amanda is appalled by men's inconstancy, Berinthia shrewdly distinguishes between the consequences of love for men and women by means of the usage of 'baby' for 'doll':

Now there's nothing upon Earth astonishes me less, when I consider what they and we are compos'd of. For Nature has made them Children, and us Babies. Now, Amanda, how we us'd our Babies, you may remember. We were mad to have 'em, as soon as we saw 'em; kist 'em to pieces, as soon as we got 'em; then pull'd off their Cloaths, saw 'em naked, and so threw 'em away. (V.ii)

Vanbrugh's consistent comic cynicism makes us sceptical about Worthy's ability, when repulsed by Amanda, to find that 'the vile, the gross desires of Flesh and Blood' have been 'in a moment turn'd to Adoration'. The facility of the phrasing matches the shallowness of the emotions. Whether promiscuously loveless, or ashamedly worthy, Vanbrugh's weak characters share a self-deception about their basic natures. Against them the dramatist opposes a natural virtue, idealized in the goodness of women, made complete here in Amanda, maliciously self-betrayed in Berinthia, and wantonly rejected by Miss Hoyden. There is also a compensating comic virtue in the abused ignorance of Sir Tunbelly Clumsey.

Deputy-lieutanent of his country and a county justice with £1,500 a year, Sir Tunbelly seeks social advancement by marrying his daughter to a peer. When Young Fashion comes a-wooing in disguise his servant, Lory, senses behind the façade of the country house the strength of Sir Tunbelly's position:

Igad, Sir, this will prove some Inchanted Castle; we shall have the Gyant come out by and by with his Club, and beat our Brains out.
(III.iii)

And though Sir Tunbelly's welcome to the supposed lord is meticulously detailed in terms of the social necessity to meet rank by ostentation, the true giant comes out like the rampant spirit of the English squirearchy in arms to bar the door against the real Foppington. Just how doomed such rural weapons are against the urbane invasion is conveyed by Foppington:

A Pax of these Bumkinly People, will they open the Gate, or do they desire I should grow at their Moat-side like a Willow? (IV.v)

The bumpkin triumphs temporarily over the foppish nobility, but the risks of sentimental comedy are skilfully avoided when both squire and noble are outwitted by youthful deceit and aged expediency.

The scene of the wedding celebration in Lord Foppington's London home builds by swift manoeuvres to an explosive climax. Miss Hoyden looks forward to her debut among hostesses who will 'laugh till they crack again, to see me slip my Collar, and run away from my Husband'. Sir Tunbelly gets drunk before supper and ogles the ladies with gleeful violence: 'Udsookers, they set my old Blood a-fire; I shall cuckold some body before Morning.' The guests listen to a masque of the contention between Cupid and Hymen, the chorus of which chants for change:

> Constancy's an empty sound.
> Heaven, and Earth, and all go round,
> All the Works of Nature move,
> And the Joys of Life and Love
>   Are in Variety.

The change comes more rapidly then even these guests predict. Young Fashion claims his wife, supported by the sacred testimony of Parson Bull and the Nurse. Clumsey stumps off in rage. Lord Foppington decides to 'put on a serene Countenance, for a Philosophical Air is the most becoming thing in the World to the face of a Person of Quality'.

But Vanbrugh's play does not end with any delight in the moral conformity of this marriage. Fashion informs his bride that his brother will be at hand and 'ready to come to' should their partnership fail, and Foppington swears devoutly, 'Her Ladyship shall stap my Vitals, if I do.'

Relapse is the condition of this changeful world, and what invites our laughter remains the spectacle of unregenerate nature. For Miss Hoyden, silent at last, stands ready to draw on the hounds like the tame hare her father so well nurtured.

ii

The Provok'd Wife, Vanbrugh's only other completed original play, usually considered his masterpiece, has a long theatrical history. It owes its popularity mainly to the opportunities which the part of Sir John Brute has given to a long succession of actors, from Betterton to Wolfit.

Brute opens the play with a stunning assault upon the tedium of a two-year-old marriage which has 'debaucht my five senses'. His wife-cursing hatred generates an immediate quarrel and establishes a basic cross purpose. 'You married me for Love,' says Lady Brute. 'And you me for Money,' he retorts.

Lady Brute is efficient at self-analysis. She had married against advice because 'I thought I had Charms enough to govern him; and that where there was an Estate, a Woman must needs be happy': it is a short paragraph from this observation to meditation upon revenge, and the persuasion that 'a good part of what I suffer from my Husband may be a Judgment upon me for my Cruelty to my Lover'; and it is a shorter step, by way of comparison between the matrimonial vow and the easy covenant of a sovereign with his people, to dramatic decision:

if I argue the matter a little longer with my self, I shan't find so many Bug-bears in the way, as I thought I shou'd. Lord what fine notions of Virtue do we Women take up upon the Credit of old foolish Philosophers. Virtue's its own reward, Virtue's this, Virtue's that— Virtue's an Ass, and a Gallant's worth forty on't. (I.i)

The direction which Lady Brute's thoughts take prepares us for the subsequent course of events in the play, which draws its dramatic tensions from the antagonisms of an incompatible marriage between characters who typify brutalized masculine conceit and natural feminine virtue. Sir John is addicted to gambling, drunkenness, and the company of roistering friends with a military swagger only equalled by their cowardice. Lady Brute is companioned by a niece, Bellinda, inexperienced enough to think she can sum up her aunt's feelings towards the loyal gallant Constant:

In a Word; never was poor Creature so spurr'd on by desire, and so rein'd in with fear.

SIR JOHN VANBRUGH
from a painting by SIR GODFREY KNELLER *for the Kit-Kat Club*
National Portrait Gallery

above: Castle Howard, Yorkshire, the south front

Grimsthorpe Castle, Lincolnshire, the Hall

Lady Brute's problem is more complex, however. She
has common sense enough to admit that 'Coquettry is one
of the main ingredients in the natural Composition of a
woman', and social sense enough to laugh at the vanity of
her neighbour, Lady Fancyfull, a desperate flirt. But when
Bellinda turns to a related subject, the jealousy of husbands,
Lady Brute has to confess that Sir John 'do's not love me
well enough for that':

Lord how wrong Men's Maxims are. They are seldom jealous of their
Wives, unless they are very fond of 'em; whereas they ought to consider
the Womans Inclinations, for there depends their Fate.   (I.i)

It is a light preface to an innocent intrigue, but it masks a
strength of purpose and a power of feeling which the play's
devices constantly arouse and subdue. Lady Brute is an
illustration, since proof is scarcely required, of D. H.
Lawrence's observation that women have 'the logic of
emotion, men have the logic of reason. The two are comple-
mentary and mostly in opposition'.

The drama of the provoked wife springs from the fact
that this 'woman's logic'—whether of Lady Brute, Lady
Fancyfull or Mademoiselle her maid—is 'no less real and
inexorable than the man's logic of reason':

She may spend years living up to a masculine pattern. But in the end,
the strange and terrible logic of emotion will work out the smashing of
that pattern, if it has not been emotionally satisfactory. This is the partial
explanation of the astonishing changes in women. For years they go on
being chaste Beatrices or child-wives. Then on a sudden—bash! The
chaste Beatrice becomes a roaring lioness! The pattern didn't suffice,
emotionally.[1]

The temptation of Lady Brute arises at once from her
own inclinations and from the exceptional willingness of
her society to provide her with a feminine pattern.
Vanbrugh's dramatic instinct shares the social impulse

[1] D. H. Lawrence, 'Give her a Pattern', *Selected Essays* (1950), p.22.

towards that final 'bash!', but his sense of comic irony contains it.

Lady Brute's feelings for Constant are intensified when she assists his friend Heartfree to court Bellinda, and they are complicated by the treacherous intriguing of Lady Fancyfull to gain Heartfree for herself, in which she is aided by her enterprising strumpet of a French maid and the enslaved Razor, Sir John's valet.

Vanbrugh's inventiveness of stage incident is at its strongest in *The Provok'd Wife*, and the effective surprises of action continually reinforce the play's overmastering irony. Thus the innocent assignation of Lady Brute and Bellinda with Constant and Heartfree in Spring Garden derives its piquancy initally from the fact that all four are being spied upon by Lady Fancyfull and her maid. But this episode of conventional intrigue is alarmingly transformed by the arrival of Sir John Brute who has been freshly released from detention, after impersonating a parson and scandalizing the constabulary, and is seeking a whore. He seizes his wife and Bellinda in disguise; they are forced to reveal themselves to their suitors so that Lady Brute may escape from her husband's ravishing attention. The exposure removes the present danger but promotes a greater. Heartfree and Constant renew their demands, strengthened by the women's duplicity, and Lady Brute, crying, 'Ah! I am lost', and forced by Constant towards a convenient arbour, is only recovered because Lady Fancyfull and her maid are driven out of the same refuge. It is a revelation that finally saves Lady Brute; her hair 'stands on end', and she and Bellinda flee.

The irony of the play is constantly illustrated in terms of physical experience. Thus, Sir John's own salvation is accomplished by an appropriate crudity of behaviour. Having arrived home drunk, and displayed insulting affection for his wife, he momentarily abandons the warmth of sexual desire for a cup of her cold tea and opens the cupboard to discover Constant and Heartfree. The anticipated savagery is skilfully dissipated by his very inebriation. 'All dirt and bloody' from his previous street scuffle he is soon overcome by fatigue and falls asleep in his chair. He is thus preserved by this surrender to his body's gross appetite from a more despicable attempt to defend a fraudulent honour by provoking a duel which he is too cowardly to fight. The denouement finds him suitably chastened.

Vanbrugh's ear in *The Provok'd Wife* is as responsive as his hand to the dramatic needs. He perfectly catches the confident masculine tone of the discussions between Heartfree and Constant, the delicacy of the exchanges between Constant and Lady Brute, or the intimacy of her talks with Bellinda. For instance, Lady Brute catechizes Constant upon his attitude to 'That Phantome of Honour', testing their opposing logic:

Lady Brute. If it be a thing of so little Value, why do you so earnestly recommend it to your Wives and Daughters?

Constant. We recommend it to our Wives, Madam, because we wou'd keep 'em to our selves. And to our Daughters, because we wou'd dispose of 'em to others.

Lady Brute. 'Tis, then, of some Importance, it seems, since you can't dispose of 'em without it.

Constant. That importance, Madam, lies in the humour of the Country, not in the nature of the thing.

Lady Brute. How do you prove that, Sir?

Constant. From the Wisdom of a neighb'ring Nation in a contrary Practice. In Monarchies things go by Whimsies, but Commonwealths weigh all things in the Scale of Reason.

Lady Brute. I hope we are not so very light a People to bring up fashions without some ground.

Constant. Pray what do's your Ladiship think of a powder'd Coat for Deep Mourning?

Lady Brute. I think, Sir, your Sophistry has all the effect that you can reasonably expect it should have: it puzzles, but don't convince.

Constant. I'm sorry for it.

Lady Brute. I'm sorry to hear you say so.

Constant. Pray why?

Lady Brute. Because if you expected more from it, you have a worse opinion of my understanding than I desire you shou'd have.

Constant (aside). I comprehend her: She would have me set a value upon her Chastity, that I may think my self the more oblig'd to her, when she makes me a Present of it.   (III.i)

Such discourse has no trace of the wit-combats of lovers in the comedy of manners, and the reputation of Vanbrugh's style has suffered both from his own admission that he wrote as he spoke and from Cibber's report that actors found 'the style of no author whatsoever gave their memory less trouble'. Yet both statements deserve to be taken as compliments to Vanbrugh's skill in language, which is particularly effective in dealing with affectation and cant. For instance, the social hypocrisy of men and women is glanced at by Lady Brute and Bellinda, who practises before her mirror 'both how to speak myself, and how to look when others speak':

Bellinda. But my Glass and I cou'd never yet agree what Face I shou'd make, when they come blurt out with a nasty thing in a Play: For all the Men presently look upon the Women, that's certain; so laugh we must not, tho' our Stays burst for't, because that's telling Truth, and owning we understand the Jest. And to look serious is so dull, when the whole House is a laughing.

Lady Brute. Besides, that looking serious do's really betray our Knowledge: For if we did not understand the thing, we shou'd naturally do like other People.

Bellinda. For my part I always use that occasion to blow my Nose.

Lady Brute. You must blow your Nose half off then at some Plays.
           (III.iii)

Bellinda asks, 'Why don't some Reformer or other beat the Poet for 't?', and Lady Brute shrewdly counters, 'Because he is not so sure of our private Approbation, as of our publick Thanks.'

Vanbrugh cleverly uses the traditional French complaint against English hypocrisy when Mademoiselle mimics with phrase and posture the encounter between Lady Brute and Constant in Spring Garden, inciting the wretched Razor to lustful complicity in love-making. He pleads, 'But why wilt thou make me such a Rogue, my Dear?', and is taunted with 'Voilà un vrai Anglois! il est amoureux, et cependant il veut raisonner. Vet en au Diable'. The desperate Razor surrenders to her plot: 'In hopes thou'lt give me up thy Body, I resign thee up my Soul.' Such comic inflation in no way diminishes the strength of their immoral defiance. Indeed the defeat of Lady Fancyfull's schemes involves more than a mechanical return to respectability. When her mask is stripped off, and her pretensions harshly exposed, she struggles to regain some human dignity. She was more deeply committed to her amorous desire than Foppington was to his proposed marriage, and she is correspondingly less successful in putting on a social face. Bellinda, seeing 'what a Passion she's in', forgives her with something of Olivia's pity for the abused Malvolio.

The Provok'd Wife concludes in mutual pardon and acknowledgement of faults. A similar tactful recognition seems required on the part of criticism, for Vanbrugh's immorality was attacked by just such a reformer as Bellinda mentioned, when Collier's Short View satirically and judiciously arraigned his plays for profanity, bawdy and the scurrilous treatment of clergy and sacred script. Vanbrugh's retort, A Short Vindication, could scarcely hope to counter these charges and ought not to have so attempted. Vanbrugh's best defence lay in fresh attack, and the brief polemic which introduced the text of The Relapse is a pungent expression of his artistic aims. Apologizing for offence given to 'any honest Gentleman of the Town, whose Friendship or good Worth is worth the having', Vanbrugh admits that he had no other design 'in running a very great Risk, than to divert (if possible) some part of their Spleen, in spite of their Wives and their Taxes', but adds 'One more word about the Bawdy':

I own the first Night this thing was acted, some Indecencies had like to have happen'd, but 'Twas not my Fault.

The fine Gentleman of the Play, drinking his Mistress's Health in

Nants Brandy, from six in the Morning to the time he waddled on upon
the Stage, had toasted himself up to such a pitch of vigour, I confess I
once gave *Amanda* for gone, and am since (with all due respect to Mrs
Rogers) very sorry she 'scapt; for I am confident a certain Lady (let no
one take it to herself that's handsome) who highly blames the Play, for
the Barrenness of the Conclusion, would then have allow'd it a very
natural Close.

Vanbrugh's plays offer more inherent offence than might
be given through the insobriety of Powell or any actor,
and it is typical that his proposed apology should erupt into
fresh insult. For the risks Vanbrugh accepted are inseparable
from his comic force and directness. Leigh Hunt passed over
The Provok'd Wife as a play 'more true than pleasant', and
though Vanbrugh prudently replaced the scene of Sir John
Brute in a priest's gown by one in which he wears his
wife's clothes, the substituted version has held the stage
since not only because it affords more continuous opportunities for topical satire, but because it strengthens the element
of sexual antagonism in Brute.[1]

The play was defended in its own time against the charge
of 'a loose Performance' when Giles Jacob discovered in its
design a utilitarian morality that 'teaches Husbands how
they are to expect their Wives Should shew a Resentment,
if they use them as Sir *John Brute* did his' (*The Poetical
Register*, 1719). It seems wiser now to content ourselves with
the position that Hazlitt adopted 'On Wit and Humour':

You cannot force people to laugh, you cannot give a reason why they
should laugh;—they must laugh of themselves, or not at all. As we laugh
from a spontaneous impulse, we laugh the more at any restraint upon
this impulse. We laugh at a thing merely because we ought not.

iii

Vanbrugh's only designedly didactic play, *Aesop*, had
its origin in Boursault's Parisian success, which Vanbrugh

[1]Garrick, who made Sir John Brute one of his greatest roles, once
satirized contemporary fashion in a hat laden with vegetables and decorated
with a pendant carrot.

did not expect would gain 'so great a victory here, since 'tis possible by fooling with his Sword, I may have turn'd the Edge on't'. The play is an interesting failure, however, if only because of Farquhar's remark in *A Discourse Upon Comedy* (1702) that Aesop was 'the first and original author' of comedy, and that 'Comedy is no more at present than a well-framed tale handsomely told as an agreeable vehicle for counsel or reproof'. It is a traditional enough argument—indeed Hazlitt, the best critic of Vanbrugh and his comic sensibility, makes Aesop central in his own exposition—and the subject ought to have occasioned good comedy. The reproving fables themselves are admirably done, and are Vanbrugh's best verse. Pope praised them:

Prior is called the English Fontaine for his tales, nothing is more unlike. But your *Fables* have the very spirit of this celebrated French poet.[1]

Vanbrugh's 'I protest to you I never read Fontaine's *Fables*', suggests the modest attention he sometimes gave to his art. The play remains an undramatic medley, enlivened by some admirable portraits: Jacob Quaint, a herald from Wales ('a Country in the World's backside, where every Man is born a Gentleman, and a Genealogist'); Mrs Forge-Will, a scrivener's widow; and, among Vanbrugh's additions, a characteristically eccentric country gentleman, Sir Polydorus Hogstye of Beast-Hall in Swine-County.

Of Vanbrugh's other adaptations from French drama, *The Country House*, a two-act farce long popular as an after-piece, now reads like a rumbustious prophecy of the fate of a stately home. It exploits the situation of Monsieur Barnard, a country squire so beset by visitors, neighbours, huntsmen and relatives that he hangs an old rusty sword at his gate for an inn sign; eventually he marries off his children, gets rid of his house and is willing to dispose of his wife too.

The headlong impetus of such a plot exuberantly displays that quality in Vanbrugh which Allardyce Nicoll terms

[1] See Austin Warren, *Alexander Pope as Critic and Humanist* (1963) for the full context of this and other references to Vanbrugh.

'buoyant with a sort of uproariousness, upheld by wine'. This is notably lacking in the two comic romances of *The False Friend* and *The Mistake*. Here intricate intrigues, though skilfully controlled, inhibit those generous tendencies of Vanbrugh's stage handling to issue into ribaldry and riot. Occasional comic moments, such as the bed-room scene in *The False Friend*, or the buffoonery with love tokens in *The Mistake*, and the energetic, pert dialogue of maids and manservants, insufficiently compensate for stock dramatic situations, and a decline in linguistic vitality.

By contrast, *The Confederacy* is a play of strong characters which displays Vanbrugh's customary gusto. Clarissa and Araminta, wives of two scriveners, Gripe and Moneytrap, join in a conspiracy against their husbands. But though the play was long popular as *The City Wives' Confederacy*, its strength lies equally in the counter-plot of Dick Amlet's pursuit of Gripe's daughter Corinna, aided by his friend Brass and the maid Flippanta, and involving the suppression of Dick's relationship with his mother, Mrs Amlet, 'a Seller of all Sorts of private Affairs to the Ladies'. The play makes a comic analysis of bourgeois greed and idleness, a shrewd revelation of the false innocence of the sixteen-year old Corinna, and a sharp caricature of snobbery in action—as Brass says to his pretended master, 'You soared up to adultery with the mistress, while I was at humble fornication with the maid'.

Yet though the play fully deserves Hazlitt's commendation as 'a comedy of infinite contrivance and intrigue, with a matchless spirit of impudence', and as 'a fine, careless *exposé* of heartless want of principle', it has the stricter virtues of French realistic comedy rather than the broader capacities of Vanbrugh's original plays. The play is necessarily more concerned with avaricious than with amorous gratification, and there is a correspondingly reduced sense of that competition of the ideal with the materialistic, the ignorant with the sophisticated, that gives a fuller life to *The Relapse* and *The Provok'd Wife*.

In the three acts and one scene that Vanbrugh completed of *A Journey to London* he returned to those enduring pre-occupations of his art. The dilemma of Monsieur Barnard is reversed. Now, in his London house, Uncle Richard awaits the arrival of his nephew, Sir Francis Headpiece, and family to take possession of the metropolis:

Forty years and two is the Age of him; in which it is computed by his Butler, his own person has drank two and thirty Ton of Ale. The rest of his Time has been employ'd in persecuting all the poor four-legg'd Creatures round, that wou'd but run away fast enough from him, to give him the high-mettled pleasure of running after them. In this noble Employ, he has broke his right Arm, his left Leg, and both his Collar-bones—Once he broke his Neck, but that did him no harm; a nimble Hedge-leaper, a Brother of the Stirrup that was by, whipt off his Horse and mended it. (I.i)

This endearing fool, married to 'a profuse young Housewife for Love, with never a Penny of Money', and finding that 'Children and Interest-Money make such a bawling about his Ears', has set off for London to be a 'Parliament-Man', and his wife 'to play off a hundred Pounds at Dice with Ladies of Quality, before breakfast'. Uncle Richard's man James gives a profusely detailed account of the hazards of their undertakings. The vanity of Lady Headpiece has 'added two Cart-Horses to the four old Geldings' to impress the town with her coach and six, and 'heavy *George* the Plow-man rides Postillion'. The coach is 'cruelly loaden' with people, trunks, boxes and the preposterous accoutrements of their ambitious journey:

for fear of a Famine, before they shou'd get to the Baiting-place, there was such Baskets of Plumbcake, Dutch-Gingerbread, Cheshire-Cheese, Naples-Biscuits, Maccaroons, Neats-Tongues, and cold boyl'd Beef—and in case of Sickness, such Bottles of Usquebaugh, Black-cherry Brandy, Cinamon-water, Sack, Tent, and Strong beer, as made the old Coach crack again . . . . for Defence of this Good Cheer, and my Lady's little Pearl Necklace, there was the Family Basket-hilt Sword, the great Turkish Cimiter, the old Blunderbuss, a good Bag of Bullets, and a great Horn of Gunpowder . . . . Then for Band-boxes, they were so bepiled up, to Sir *Francis's* Nose, that he cou'd only peep out at a chance Hole with one Eye, as if he were viewing the Country thro' a Perspective-Glass.

This clearly was the task that Vanbrugh set himself as dramatist, sweeping his perspective-glass round the range of contemporary social circumstances and attitudes. His observation took in a series of disintegrating personal and social partnerships. The innocent Sir Francis is drawn to London only to be disillusioned by the true nature of parliamentary patronage; the scheming Lady Headpiece is seduced by the world of Colonel Courtly and the gaming-table fraternity; Arabella Loverule's spirited claims for personal freedom grow uncontrollably towards the condition of total irresponsibility.

For the Loverules Vanbrugh provided his finest marital quarrel, unquotable because its entirety is needed to demonstrate its compulsive rhythmic growth. And in the conversation of Lord Loverule and Sir Charles on the subject of divorce Vanbrugh found a vocabulary for a hitherto inarticulated sensibility. They look back upon their idealized adoration of women, and contemplate the prospect of reversal:

Lord Loverule.   And what Relief?
Sir Charles.   A short one; leave it, and return to that you left, if you can't find a better.
Lord Loverule.   He says right—that's the Remedy, and a just one—for if I sell my Liberty for Gold, and I am foully paid in Brass, shall I be held to keep the Bargain? (*Aside*)
Sir Charles.   What are you thinking of?
Lord Loverule.   Of what you have said.
Sir Charles.   And was it well said?
Lord Loverule.   I begin to think it might.
Sir Charles.   Think on, 'twill give you Ease—the Man who has courage enough to part with a Wife, need not much dread the having one; and he that has not ought to tremble at being a Husband.   (II.i)

Lord Loverule believes that '(tho' the Misfortunes's great) he'll make a better Figure in the World, who keeps an ill Wife out of Doors, than he that keeps her within'. Colley Cibber reports that what Vanbrugh 'intended in the *Catastrophe*, was, that the Conduct of his Imaginary Fine Lady had so provok'd him, that he design'd actually to have made her Husband turn her out of his Doors'. But when Cibber completed the play he transformed this intention in the interest of reconciliation and the terms of sentimental comedy; just as Sheridan was to dilute the ribald energy of *The Relapse* in *A Trip to Scarborough*. Vanbrugh himself could not accomplish his design, and his unfinished masterpiece of *A Journey to London* ends, as his own life did, in an apoplectic hiatus:

> *Lady Headpiece.* What do you mean, Sir *Francis*, to disturb the Company, and abuse the Gentleman thus?
>
> *Sir Francis.* I mean to be in a Passion.
>
> *Lady Headpiece.* And why will you be in a passion, Sir *Francis*?
>
> *Sir Francis.* Because I came here to Breakfast with my Lady there, before I went down to the House, expecting to find my Family set round a civil Table with her, upon some Plumb Cake, hot Roles, and a cup of Strong Beer; instead of which, I find these good Women staying their Stomachs with a Box and Dice, and that Man there, with the strange Perriwig, making a good hearty Meal upon my Wife and Daughter—

It is a revealing moment for Vanbrugh's art to have faltered, and eventually to have fallen silent. He possessed neither the passionate ferocity of Wycherley nor the satirical intelligence of Congreve, either of whom would have accomplished a dramatic solution for Vanbrugh's dilemma. Vanbrugh seems to have remained undecided between the resources of natural wit and cheerful violence, which would have led him to a characteristically explosive denouement, and a new seriousness of mind, represented here in the conversation of Sir Charles and Lord Loverule, and owed perhaps to the example of Farquhar's *The Beaux' Stratagem*.

Vanbrugh and Farquhar are certainly near to each other

in time, dramatic themes, and theatrical techniques, and their plays have more in common than the work of any other two dramatists of the Restoration period. Neither is much concerned with earlier preoccupations of Restoration comedy, such as witty heroines, gay couples and the strict delineation of fashion; both manage to balance town sophistication with provincial vitality, and find the centre of dramatic interest in marriage as much as in courtship. But there remains an important dissimilarity. Whereas *The Beaux' Stratagem* refines upon *The Provok'd Wife*, and seeks for a change in the social attitude towards divorce, Vanbrugh's play reaches a conclusion in terms of personal freedom beyond the law. Farquhar, had he lived, might have managed the transition between the attitudes of the Restoration dramatists and those of the Sentimentalists who succeeded them; he might indeed have given some of his strength and vivacity to their often maudlin morality.

By contrast, Vanbrugh's whole art was created in response to the tendency towards sentimentalism which he discerned in Colley Cibber, and thrived in a decade dominated by farce. But Vanbrugh was not so much incapable of refinement—the frequent idealization of women indicate the possibility—as manfully resistant to it. Indeed, his qualities seem curiously inseparable from his weaknesses. His best plays survive, and are still powerfully effective, because their basic themes appeal to common sense and to the common senses alike. In the eighteenth century his plays often suffered adaptation and false refinement; in the nineteenth century they were frequently reduced to their farcical elements, and performed episodically; in the twentieth century *The Relapse* has been adapted as a popular musical comedy. Yet Vanbrugh's honesty of viewpoint remains. If he had sustained his gaze upon human behaviour it would have proved essentially disconcerting.

Indeed, had he completed *A Journey to London* Vanbrugh might have exemplified Coleridge's maxim that 'Farce is nearer Tragedy in its Essence than Comedy is'.

III. A POET AS WELL AS AN ARCHITECT

> Under this stone, reader, survey
> Dead Sir John Vanbrugh's house of clay.
> Lie heavy on him, earth! for he
> Laid many heavy loads on thee.

Abel Evans's epitaph is fitter to begin a comment upon
Vanbrugh's architecture with than to end it; for, though he
would have been the first to appreciate its wit, we ought to
be the last to endorse it. Because it is the activity, not the
inertness, of Vanbrugh's buildings that most imposes itself
upon the spectator's eye, whether trained or untrained,
devout or derisive.

Vanbrugh's amateur status as an architect, and his professional reputation as a wit, made him a fair target for
others' witticisms. His Whitehall home was mocked by
Swift as 'A thing resembling a Goose-pie', and the progress
of his art was described from the time when

> Van's genius ,without thought or lecture,
> Is hugely turn'd to architecture:

with passing reference to its inspiration in children's mud
games, until

> From such deep rudiments as these,
> Van is become, by due degrees,
> For building famed, and justly reckon'd,
> At court Vitruvius the second.
> (*The History of Van's House*, 1708)

The jest rankled. Swift reported to Stella on 7 November,
1710 that Vanbrugh 'had a long quarrel with me about those
Verses on his House; but we were very civil and cold. Lady
Marlborough used to teaze with him, which made him
angry, though he be a good-natured fellow'.

Vanbrugh could expect such sallies from his political
opponents, particularly in view of Pope's friendship with

Lady Marlborough, and his own creation of Eastbury Park
for Pope's victim Bubb Doddington.

At Vanbrugh's death Swift and Pope repented in a joint-
preface to their *Miscellanies* of 1727:

> In Regard to Two Persons only we wish our Railery, though ever so
> tender, or Resentment, though ever so just, had not been indulged.
> We speak of Sir John Vanbrugh, who was a Man of Wit, and of Honour,
> and of Mr Addison, whose Name deserves all Respect from every Lover
> of Learning.

The company he keeps in this epitaph would have pleased
the gregarious Vanbrugh, whom Pope depicted as 'the most
easy, careless writer and companion in the world . . . who
wrote and built just as his fancy led him, or as those he built
for and wrote for directed him'.

There is a sense, however, in which, literally, Pope and
Swift did not know what they were talking about.
Vanbrugh was no Vitruvius. But he was, with Wren and
Nicholas Hawksmoor, the architect of a school of Baroque
that lasted for little more than a generation in England,
which had to wait for Horace Walpole before it received
aesthetic admiration, and for Sir Joshua Reynolds' Thir-
teenth Discourse, of December 11, 1786, for any authorit-
ative discernment of critical principles.

Vanbrugh's reputation can no longer stand apart from
Hawksmoor's; Sir John Summerson sums up a continuing
scholarly enquiry as follows:

> The truth can only be that *both* Hawksmoor *and* Vanbrugh were very
> exceptional men; that they exploited the same sources in continuous
> mutual discussion, and shared, more fully, perhaps, then either knew,
> each other's treasuries of knowledge and invention.[1]

With this qualification prominently stated it is still
possible to find in Sir Joshua Reynolds' seulogy some of the
terms still valuable for the appreciation of an architecture

[1] *Architecture in Britain: 1530–1830* (1963), p.168.

both heroic and human, grandly placed and intimately detailed.

Reynolds paid tribute to Vanbrugh 'in the language of a Painter', as an architect who perfectly 'understood in his Art what is the most difficult in ours, the conduct of the background':

What the background is in Painting, in Architecture is the real ground on which the building is erected; and no Architect took greater care than he that his work should not appear crude and hard; that is, it did not start abruptly out of the ground without expectation of preparation.

Reynolds understood Vanbrugh's concern with light and shadow, exemplified in his treatment of exterior and interior arcades, his spectacular development of emphasis in approach, and admired, above all, those poetic towers and battlements which painters and poets 'make a part of the composition of their ideal landscape':

it is from hence in a great degree, that in the buildings of Vanbrugh, who was a Poet as well as an Architect, there is a greater display of imagination, than we shall find perhaps in any other.

SIR JOHN VANBRUGH

A Select Bibliography

(Place of publication London, unless stated otherwise. Detailed bibliographical information will also be found in the appropriate volumes of *The Cambridge Bibliography of English Literature* and *The Oxford History of English Literature*.)

Bibliography:

A CHECK LIST OF ENGLISH PLAYS, 1641–1700, by G. L. Woodward and J. G. McManaway, Chicago (1945).

Collected Works:

THE COMPLETE WORKS OF SIR JOHN VANBRUGH, the plays edited by B. Dobrée, the letters by G. Webb, 4 vols (1927–8)
—the standard edition, limited to 1,410 copies. Vols I–III contain all Vanbrugh's plays, including his version of Fletcher's *The Pilgrim* and Cibber's *The Provok'd Husband*, and omitting only the dubious *Squire Trelooby;* also printed is Vanbrugh's *A Short Vindication.* Vol. IV contains the majority of Vanbrugh's letters, edited from transcripts, together with certain documents relating to Blenheim.

PLAYS, WRITTEN BY SIR JOHN VANBRUGH, 2 vols (1719)
—this first 'collected edition' lacks *The Country House* and precedes publication of *A Journey to London,* added in 1730 and 1734.

PLAYS, WRITTEN BY SIR JOHN VANBRUGH, 2 vols (1735).

THE DRAMATIC WORKS OF WYCHERLEY, CONGREVE, VANBRUGH AND FARQUHAR, ed. Leigh Hunt (1840)
—omits Cibber's *The Provok'd Husband.*

THE PLAYS OF SIR JOHN VANBRUGH, ed. W. C. Ward, 2 vols (1893)
—omits Cibber's *The Provok'd Husband.*
   Note: *The Pilgrim* is omitted from all eighteenth-century and nineteenth-century collected editions.

Selections:

SIR JOHN VANBRUGH, ed. A. E. H. Swaen (1896)
—contains *The Relapse, The Provok'd Wife, The Confederacy, A Journey to London.*

RESTORATION PLAYS FROM DRYDEN TO FARQUHAR (1912)
—includes *The Provok'd Wife*.

Separate Works:

THE RELAPSE, OR VIRTUE IN DANGER (1696)
—title-page 1697; frequently reprinted and collected; edited by D. MacMillan and M. H. Jones in *Plays of the Restoration and Eighteenth Century* (1931). Adapted as *A Man of Quality*, by Lee, 1776; as *A Trip to Scarborough*, by R. B. Sheridan, 1781.

AESOP (1697)
—Part I and Part II were published separately in 1697, then in a combined edition of the same year.

THE PROVOK'D WIFE (1697)
—frequently reprinted; the 1743 (Dublin) text contains Act IV, Scene i and Scene iii, as Vanbrugh rewrote them for performance in 1706; collections frequently give these as additions.

A SHORT VINDICATION OF THE RELAPSE AND THE PROVOK'D WIFE FROM IMMORALITY AND PROPHANENESS, BY THE AUTHOR (1698)

THE PILGRIM (1700)
—the title-page continues 'A Comedy, as it is acted at the Theatre-Royal, in Drury Lane. Written originally by Mr Fletcher, and now very much alter'd, with several additions. Likewise a prologue epilogue, dialogue and masque, written by the late great poet Mr Dryden, just before his death, being the last of his works.

THE FALSE FRIEND (1702)
—adapted as *Friendship à la Mode*, Dublin, 1766.

TO A LADY MORE CRUEL THAN FAIR (1704)
—verses first printed in Tonson's *Dryden's Miscellany*, Fifth Part 1704.

THE CONFEDERACY (1705)
—adapted from Dancourt's *Les Bourgeoises à la Mode*. Often acted as *The City Wives Confederacy*.

THE MISTAKE (1706)
—a version of *Le Dépit Amoureux* by Molière. Adapted as *Lovers Quarrels, or Like Master Like Man*, by T. King, Dublin, 1770.

THE COUNTRY HOUSE (1715)
—reprinted as *La Maison Rustique, or the Country House*, 1740.

SIR JOHN VANBRUGH'S JUSTIFICATION OF WHAT HE DEPOS'D IN THE DUKE OF MALRBOROUGH'S LATE TRYAL (1721).

A JOURNEY TO LONDON (1728)

—unfinished play, afterwards completed by Cibber, as *The Provok'd Husband.*

THE PROVOK'D HUSBAND; OR, A JOURNEY TO LONDON, by Sir J. Vanbrugh and C. Cibber (1728)

SQUIRE TRELOOBY (1704)

—an adaptation by Congreve, Vanbrugh and Walsh of Molière's *Monsieur de Pourceaugnac;* the translators, however, repudiated the text of another *Monsieur de Pourceaugnac, or 'Squire Trelooby',* attributed to John Ozell and also printed 1704: see J. C. Hodges, ' "The Authorship of" *Squire Trelooby', Review of English Studies,* 4, 1928, 404–13.

THE CUCKOLD IN CONCEIT (presumed unprinted.)

—acted 1707

Biographical Studies:

ESSAYS IN BIOGRAPHY, by B. Dobrée (1925)

—the main materials for Vanbrugh's life are to be found here and in the same author's Introduction to *The Complete Works.*

SIR JOHN VANBRUGH, ARCHITECT AND DRAMATIST, 1664–1726, by L. Whistler (1938)

—a brilliant, sympathetic and full appraisal.

Architectural Studies:

THE IMAGINATION OF VANBRUGH AND HIS FELLOW ARTISTS, by L. Whistler (1954)

—a near-definitive account, superbly illustrated and documented, including additional letters.

HAWKSMOOR, by K. Downes (1959).

THE WORKS OF SIR JOHN VANBRUGH AND HIS SCHOOL, 1699–1736, by H. A. Tipping (1928)

—Vol. II in *English Homes, Period IV.*

THE WREN SOCIETY: Vols I-XX, ed. A. T. Bolton and H. D. Hendry (1924–44).

ARCHITECTURE IN BRITAIN: 1530–1830, by John Summerson (1953)

—fourth edition, revised and enlarged, 1963.

A BIOGRAPHICAL DICTIONARY OF ENGLISH ARCHITECTS, 1660–1840, by H. M. Colvin (1945)
—contains a concise check-list of Vanbrugh's buildings.

SURVEY OF LONDON, Vols XXIX and XXX (1960)
—important account of Vanbrugh's Haymarket Opera House; but see further a review by R. Leacroft, *Theatre Notebook*, XVI, 1, 1961.

Some Critical Studies:

A SHORT VIEW OF THE IMMORALITY AND PROFANENESS OF THE STAGE, by J. Collier (1698).

AN APOLOGY FOR THE LIFE OF MR COLLEY CIBBER, BY HIMSELF (1740)
—standard edition, 2 vols ed. R. W. Lowe (1889).

LECTURES ON THE ENGLISH COMIC WRITERS (LECTURE IV), by W. Hazlitt (1819).

A HISTORY OF ENGLISH DRAMA, 1660–1900, by A. Nicoll Vol. I (1923) and Vol. II (1925)
—the standard critical history, with supplementary check lists and stage documents. Vol. I, fourth edition revised, 1961; Vol. II, third edition revised, 1952.

STROLLING PLAYERS & DRAMA IN THE PROVINCES, 1660–1765, by S. Rosenfeld, Cambridge (1939).

BEAUMONT AND FLETCHER ON THE RESTORATION STAGE, by A. C. Sprague (1926)
—contains an analysis of Vanbrugh's handling of Fletcher's *The Pilgrim*.

DAVID GARRICK: DIRECTOR, by K. A. Burnim, Pittsburgh (1961)
—reconstructs the stage business of Garrick's *The Provok'd Wife*.

THE COMEDY OF MANNERS, by J. Palmer (1913).

RESTORATION COMEDY, 1660–1720, by B. Dobrée (1924).

COMEDY AND CONSCIENCE AFTER THE RESTORATION, by J. W. Krutch, New York, (1924)
—enlarged edition, 1949. A useful wide-ranging account, including a discussion of the controversy between the companies.

THE COMIC SPIRIT IN THE RESTORATION DRAMA, by H. T. E. Perry, New Haven (1925)
—still one of the most effective and attractive criticisms of Vanbrugh and his contemporaries.

'A Re-evaluation of Vanbrugh', by P. Mueschke and J. Fleisher, in PMLA, Vol XLIX (1934)
—a detailed study deserving particular attention.

RESTORATION THEATRE, ed. J. R. Brown and B. Harris, Stratford-upon-Avon Studies, 6, 1965.

ENGLISH COMIC DRAMA, by F. W. Bateson (1929)
—valuable for Cibber and the post-Vanbrugh drama.

COMEDY AND SOCIETY FROM CONGREVE TO FIELDING, by J. Loftis, Stanford (1959)
—contains useful historical and comparative reference.

A CENTURY OF ENGLISH FARCE, by L. Hughes (1956)
—especially relevant reading for the decade 1696–1706, the period of Vanbrugh's dramatic activity.